FOR US

For Us

**DAVID
RIVAS-TORRES**

Ingram Spark

First Printing, 2024

Dedication

To you,
Thank you for allowing me to love you as deeply as I can.

To my younger self,
We did it, we're an author!

To my readers,
May these poems do for you what the poetry of others
has done for me.
May these words serve as a refuge in times of darkness, a source of
solace in moments of despair, and a celebration of the human
experience in all its complexity.
May you find echoes of your own journey within these verses, and
may they remind you that you are never alone.

With love and empathy,
David

"In this part of the story I am the one who
Dies, the only one, and I will die of love because I love you,
Because I love you, Love, in fire and blood."

—Pablo Neruda, *Cien Sonetos de Amor*

Table of Contents

My beloved
You
Chopin's Nocturne No.20
Wine, and You
Lethe
In the forest
Transcendence
In the waves
Somewhere in the pines
Language of the earth
My mirror love
Piano riffs
Camper Van
Juniper II
Breakneck Ridge
As I age
Over the bricks
If you forget me
Elysia
Oneirataxia (*n.*
Eonian
Ballet Music Box
[Untitled]
Waves with you
December
Magic
Unwritten
Man in the glass bottle
In the cosmos
Stones
For You
September
Luscinia (M.

Black Butterfly
Slow dance
Purple perfume
Demon art
Immortal
il tuo nome
Flower-walker
[Untitled, 2]
Luna
Hands of God
L'amour de ma vie
Library-eyes
Fever dream
Amaranthine love
Nefelibata
Red Thread
Between the stars
Just be
Why we swim
Sunflower
Train car
Wild Geese
As always
Broken Heart Soliloquy
The next morning
Wildfire
Below the surface
Labyrinth
(???)
For us

My beloved

The riverbed flows shallow over smooth rocks
worn down by the current, and for a moment I know them.

River murmurs reverberate within
and if I close my eyes, beloved,
I can see you.

You've crossed the sandbars
and reached the banks with a stone in your hand,
a stone
that is perfect for your shadowbox.

But if I open my eyes, Sweet Love you are gone.
You are not standing
on the deep-stained wood porch that we fell in love with
on the cabin,
in the woods of Snohomish.
Your elegance
is not framed by the Washington pines,
and our hounds do not howl for me to cross the water.

There will be no long nights
filled
with red-orange glows and crackling beneath bricks,
and there will be no early August mornings with heavy air
damp from the tree roots.

Perhaps, one day
we'll meet here again, and our eyes
will both be open.

"on the deep-stained wood porch that we fell in love with

on the cabin,

in the woods of Snohomish"

You

I have loved before
and then I have loved *you.*

I was in love—
with the way that you danced in the moonlight naked
beneath the stars,
the wind your waist-wrapped partner.
You counted time in whispers as I watched with wonder,
your pirouette before the leaves.

You bathed before the breeze,
strands of hair and wind caught against your portrait,
you were
porcelain and marble-in-motion in the night.

I was locked into your fairy-twirls
in
the navy blue grass below the shadows of the trees. Your
feet gripped the ground
as you spun in swirls and I thought
I am in love.

There will always be lake-tides
that reach out for the shore,
and
I will always miss *you.*

"You bathed before the breeze"

Chopin's Nocturne No.20

You tasted of poetry in a garden library,
tucked behind wild grape vines
in secret.

You were the sunflower who splashed
against the grayscale;
the nebula among us.

We loved beneath a light gray rain
on a forgotten canvas,
in colors
of blended ocean blues darkened
by storms and haze.

I crave you
as the mountains crave the heavens,
and I miss you
in the pains of pianos.

"and I miss you
in the pains of pianos"

Wine, and You

I wonder with the wolves yes,
it's true.
We drink wine and toast to:
hand-bound moleskins with magic and
entombed love letters in weathered leather spines.

Do you recall?

Getting lost in the covers, creating new colors?
I hope you have discovered
someone who holds you tighter,
someone to paint with,
and
someone to stoke your fire.

I could never tire of the music you are to me.

You were my melody in the morning,
and you are still
my heart that is storming.

There are galactic gaps in the world that run me through,
and I fear
we'll live with unanswered questions, it's true.

If only I could taste one last time
both this wine, and You.

"If only I could taste one last time
both this wine, and You"

Lethe

I have walked to the water and watched it flow,
I have wailed with the waves, and
now I know:
If I leave, you will go, so…

Bathe me in the Lethe river and wash my memory,
drown me in forgetfulness, baptize me in the sea.
I have followed the breeze, so please, sever my soul from the soul
of the beautiful Annabel Lee.

"Bathe me in the Lethe river and wash my memory"

In the forest

In the quiet of the trees,
in the shadow of the breeze above the break
beyond the bounding seas,
I can best the barrier fog and to a small degree,
I remember *you.*

I cannot recall the shade of your eyes
nor the pierce of your laugh, and I cannot remember,
the time I saw you last.

I fear that as our time has passed
my memory has gone and crashed, a clash against my will.
I am lost in this forest without you and still,
I ride on through.

I fear I will forget,
if your eyes were brown or blue.
I cannot extract the exact scent,
that reminds me
of you.
It's a tease that it may be
bourbon vanilla beans, because I may just never know
in these woods full of dreams.

The watercolor-blends of your face
have
blurred the freckles I used to trace,
and you
have faded with time.

"in these woods full of dreams"

Transcendence

I dream during the day and dare I say,
you are still magic.

If I cover my ears I can still hear you,
your voice is carried by violins.
You say my name and you sing
I love you.

If I close my eyes I can still see you,
you are, *transcendence.*

Perhaps the memories of you are penance, perhaps,
it depends on the gods intentions.

I paint you in my poems so I never forget,
I have lost you.

"your voice is carried by violins"

In the waves

—I could stare at the waves
all the days of my days it's true;
There's something in the way
that the decades decay, all but *you*.
And time may haze the mind in grays, but—

"I could stare at the waves all the days of my days"

Somewhere in the pines

If it was love that could have saved us
then
we'd have lived forever,
somewhere in the pines perhaps or,
simply somewhere together.
And
I'd wager that the weather
would be our means to measure,
whatever increments of time crawled by.

We'd fall asleep
to gentle rainfall that pats the riverbed below,
after
we'd watched the orange light fall slow beneath the glow
of the moon.

Sound in our dreams, we'd swoon
to the tunes of the cicadas and the crickets,
enveloped in the moods of the magical thicket
we would
drift amongst the dreamy minutes, together.

The sun shines somewhere in the pines,
and I am with *you*.

"somewhere in the pines,
and I am with you"

Language of the earth

Hear me sing for you, my love,
in the rivers that rush over the rocks.
Bathe yourself in the apricots and saffrons
of my love;
In the woodsy sunlight that paints the spaces between the pines.

Sauté with snakes of light that reflect off the lakes,
for they dance as my heart does— for you.

"with snakes of light that reflect off the lakes"

My mirror love

I loved you in the shadows
when
you deserved the sun,
and now
I'm left to the jealousy of what could have been but is done.

They say mirrors hold dimensions,
and I'm sure
there's one that exists where you and I persist.

I pass the glass and I can see us
in the mountains, and in the woods. Or
well,
wouldn't that life be good?

I lie myself to bliss because I miss you
my mirror love.

"They say mirrors hold dimensions"

Piano riffs

Acoustic chords and piano riffs
sift through the wind when I think of you.
Do you miss me?

In the silence of alone,
when you're on your own at home, can you hear the harps?
They play softly in whispers:
"Do you miss her?"

I answer the music in quiet melodies
with my pen,
through ink I think, is when
I sing best.
I can feel the music in my bones
and
I can see the notes. I know I'm getting close.

Maybe this time I'll find the words.
Maybe.

"Acoustic chords and piano riffs
sift through the wind"

Camper Van

I've stood at the tip of the needle and watched the sky darken.
I've traced river bends that never end and
walked through Seikei gardens.
Your ghost refuses bargains,
please,
pardon my mistakes,
take me with you in your camper van.

I could search the margins for a parton's pull like yours
but,
foreign allure would fall short I'm sure.

I want to be with you, but I imagine and I hope—

that
you're on the road and you're in love.
that
you travel to the trees and that,
you don't take notice of how the memory of us leaves.

I should have gone with you
in that camper van.
Can
I take it back?

"Can

I take it back?"

Juniper II

Show me the way again
and I'll follow you to the water;
Two auteurs in our little boat,
who could know what we might hope?

You say
"Stroke broader in the boat now,
so we can make it to the island."

But,
can you paint me as I paddle?
Remember me in vivid color battles,
in ways I don't deserve, in
ways that preserve the moments
that we'd stolen.
Reserve a piece of your heart for me forever.
I'm afraid,
we may never reach the shore together.
If I would have known it was the last time
I would have—

stayed a little longer.
laughed a little louder.
loved a little harder.
paddled back a little slower…

"stayed a little longer.
laughed a little louder.
loved a little harder.
paddled back a little slower..."

Breakneck Ridge

Graffiti on the stone:
"No matter where we go, I'll still love you."
Perhaps you've outgrown us but
I still remember you.

You spoke of autumn and our love,
of
dying leaves and birds on the migratory breeze.
You said it hurt.

The seasons have changed
and the years have estranged us, but
I daydream of *you.*

Breakneck Ridge hikes hold you close to me:
I see you climb the rock
and I see you fawn
over the yellow in the leaves.

The spray painted stone may fade,
and the carved-in trunks on the trees may decay
but I'm afraid I still love you.

"Breakneck Ridge hikes hold you close to me"

As I age

As you grow old will you remember?
Would you still feel what we felt
and
will there still be embers?
If every day I wrote you letters,
would you still feel the fire?
Or would you remember
that we said our time together would expire?

Because I think that we stole whole moments and memories
the best we could, and would you believe,
I've watched the years flow through me as I age
and still *I love you.*

"If every day I wrote you letters"

Over the bricks

If I had to speak about love
I'd sing about us;
the whispers, the different liquors,
watching our time together flicker…

I'd reminisce:
Our walk through downtown over the bricks,
tucked-under-the-cover twists,
our double-drunken kiss.

If I had to speak about love I'd tell them
about *you.*

"I'd reminisce:
Our walk through downtown over the bricks"

If you forget me

Well, then the trees would willow
below charcoal clouds;
onyx-stained rain would rip down upon the ground,
and i would hollow.

Early morning coffees would die
before they could cool enough to sip,
and dreams of a reading nook
would wash away.

But
even if you forget me, I will always remember,
the
creaky wood beneath our feet in little bookstores,
stingray tanks in Arizona aquariums
and *you.*

"the

creaky wood beneath our feet in little bookstores"

Elysia

It has been
since before there was moss on the stones
that I have seen those eyes,
that I have bathed in the softness
of their
browns and bronzes.

I crave the days spent suspended
in the warm honey of your love,
in the wind chimes of
I love you.

I have walked the world
barefoot in the forests, in the woods;
and yet the fields remain hidden from me.

Perhaps,
I am not meant for *you,*
Elysia.

"since before there was moss on the stones"

Oneirataxia (*n.*)

because without you here with me
I think,
"Perhaps I'm stuck, in the *in-between*"

"the in-between"

Eonian

I cannot seem to find you again,
yet my love for you is eternal.

Where is it that you have gone?

I have followed
the soft whispers in my dreams,
and
they have led me to a strange fractured land, to skies of red.
They have led me
to more than one *Little Free Library,*
yet I find only myself sitting there
forgotten,
overcast in overgrown wildflowers.

I have spoken with the ocean for long enough,
and I have whispered to the winds
for far too many years;
It would seem they have fallen for you too.

"they have led me to a strange fractured land, to skies of red"

Ballet Music Box

Heartbreak is days sewn together slow, its
aching in the bones, its
bits of home simply, gone.
I wind up the ballet music box I own,
it reminds me of your gypsy hands and I know
that I'm alone.

The mornings
when you kiss my shoulders and lie still between alarms
are over.
I can't circumvent your vacuum in space
and I can't forget.

I wind up the ballet music box I own,
because she dances and I speak with you—
Thank you, I tell her as she slowly spins.

And so the ballet music box I own stops dancing
and the music fades.
This heartbreak
is days sewn slow, we could be together
but we'll never know.

"the ballet music box I own"

[Untitled]

I have buried you in my bones
and still,
you are gone.

"you are gone"

December

Who was the first to lie of heartbreak?
To say, *time will heal this wound.*
Who lied, to try to hide the truth?

December,
I miss you in the rain showers where I see your silhouette.
Beneath the lashing storm that is dense with regret
I weep, with the willows wet.

You are on loop in my heart's cassette,
where
different versions of you and I lock together
in a minuet.

I watch as we step,
in time with the time in a grayed vignette.

Perhaps for you I will fade and yet I won't forget,
that December day.

"Beneath the lashing storm that is dense with regret,
I weep, with the willows wet"

Magic

You believed in the magic around us.
You found enchantments in the canvas,
in the coffee mugs and gardens,
in
the rain strikes against the leaves.
You saw spells; You believed in *me*
and I am sorry.

"in the coffee mugs and gardens"

Unwritten

Locked in shadows and left to dust-over,
rusted hinges on our enclosure. If we could just,
trust in the great Composer, perhaps we'd not be crushed.

We have
unexplored chapters, photos left un-captured.
I simply want more.
There are pages that have not been read, and points on the paper
where the ink has bled.

We have remained, unwritten.

*"We have
unexplored chapters"*

Man in the glass bottle

Paper cranes in the sky,
and origami boats that flow down the river
into the unknown.
Paper toads leap across roads and
they go down the river
into the woodsy oaks that groan in the wind.
And hand-folded trees lean in the breeze,
while woven wild flowers stand staring at the paper leaves,
that go down the river
into the land forged by clay and hand.

At last,
the artist leans into his instruments to craft
paper-maché mills, rooted atop marbled hills
and alas, his time has passed.

He climbs into the bottle and looks through the glass:

Strong yellows pierce tired wheat fields
and the sun retires before the moon.
Colors of blueberry-silver come soon while he floats
down the river
to drown in his hopes.

"origami boats that flow down the river"

In the cosmos

The universe is expanding and
I'm sure
that somewhere out there I am standing, with you.
The cosmos grow and I just know—
somewhere out there we grow old.

If I tear through space I'm sure I'd face
myself gone mad in blues.
I'd be sure to find a me sometime, right beside *you*.

There are versions of me out there,
and
I am the poet who bleeds, for you.
He is the author who writes volumes, for you.
They are the artists who paint works, for you.

We may part ways but the forces in play don't choose,
I'll see you in the cosmos.

"I'll see you in the cosmos"

Stones

White-noise waves and morning swells
bind me in their briny spells and wash away the murky sea.
Beyond the seaweed lies,
a spell that weaves with tides that rise:
a memory of you and me.

We stood knee-deep beyond the shore, skipping rocks evermore.
And though we did ignore our ravens
finding haven in the stones,
we now reside in nevermore, rich in gothic tones.

I am on my own and so
I skip one last stone and watch it go:

A symbol of the love we used to know,
as I stand here all alone with nothing to show
but a handful of stones
and a heart full of woe.

"as I stand here all alone"

For you

Lakes coast the waters of my memory
and I'm taken to the rock,
keep me here, with you.
Every path brings me to the trees, please just
grab me, and don't let go.
Early-morning rain storms through me;
Oh, if we could just escape!
Red rays descend down to the waters,
gales of wind brush against me and
everything, reminds me of you.

"*red rays descend down to the waters*"

September

Another kiss before you leave please
and just.
one more moment before you go.
Maybe,
we can go for another walk in the woods?
We don't have to say anything,
we can just let the quiet crunches of the leaves
drown the words that hurt.

I think that I'd like for us to walk somewhere
that we need to drive to,
just so we can sing in the car one last time.
Do you think
that we could walk a little slower?

Maybe you can bring that disposable camera,
The one that you keep in your bag for *just in case,*
and I can watch you snap it at the skyline;
You never could resist a sunrise.

And when we finish our last walk together,
I hope that we can fall asleep in the way that I love the most—
you know,
when you tuck into me, below my chin and
beneath the covers in the crisp cold of the room.

I wish there was a way,
for just one more September.

"You never could resist a sunrise"

Luscinia (M.

I boarded rowboats and Vaporettos
along the emerald waters of the Venetian canals,
passing through istrian stones and stucco cements, as I searched
for you.

I traveled—
through the last of the wild grapevines
and,
past the oaks and pines,
where
I found the rolling plains from my dreams.

I could not help
but be drawn to the song before me,
for the wind called my name in your voice.

I perched myself
where I thought that you might have loved to be,
and when I closed my eyes
I thought of you.

Oh!
How I wish that I could sing, *il tuo nome...*
il tuo nome...

Yet
the gods have bound my beak in barbed wire,
for
I am not meant to hum hymns
without *you.*

"I perched myself
where I thought that you might have loved to be"

Black Butterfly

We would not stop for the black butterfly,
but he could stop for us.
We tried to hide behind the butterflies in blue,
hoping that he'd crystallize or be hypnotized by the omens,
by the motions of emotions but still he fluttered right on through.

We thought perhaps
the drumming of the monarch flaps,
might spare us another moment.
And we hoped by chance for one last dance
before inevitable atonement.

It would seem even butterflies of green,
would not be strong enough to stand between
us
and that black butterfly.

And so before this fate we stood as he approached,
he beat his black wings at us, their depth a dark riposte.
His anger
swallowed whole our souls and made a promise we could trust:
we would not live to see another day,
and our story would be dust.

"the drumming of the monarch flaps"

Slow dance

We slow danced in a burning room,
beside flames,
beneath smoke plumes.
Embers singed us and our skin sang slow-turning tunes.

The fire around us consumed all
but my love for you.
Still
we danced until my hands left your waist bruised—

I couldn't let you go.

"The fire around us consumed all
but my love for you"

Purple perfume

Poignant aromas roll lowly across the floor,
s l o w l y d r i f t i n g . . .
spreading wholly and tolling heartache from below your door.
Your venom is perfume,
it wisps itself and coils,
the toxic blanket persists and toils and I
i n h a l e.

Noxious vapors burn
and
the air is thick with layers, and I've grown sick.
Our house creaks in pain and it rains, in plums and poisons.

I'm not sure what I see,
I'm not sure what I breathe.
These spores are yours,
they pump purple in the *b r e e z e.*

"Your venom is perfume"

Demon art

The sun lifts its head, it's dawning.
Yawning, the morning's light is red.
The world is cast in scarlet by the demon artist,
he's impressed with how he's started.

The grass is darker crimson and the trees
a lighter rose,
The wind blows a blush, as it flows with no rush
beyond the blood seas.

The tides crash apple
and his eyes remember Eve.
His paint strokes soften as his pallet colors weave.
He pulls another hue and soon
the red leaves.

The bristles dip in deep ocean blue.
His hand follows the motion
of the lyrics of his spirit, and his paint is born anew.

Violet clouds birth a lavender shade,
and the canvas day showers
purple rain.

"beyond the blood seas"

Immortal

When the day breaks and eventide skies wash in,
navy blues blend with blacks in cosmic
caracola-spirals.

The silver dress of the sad
sad moon,
shimmers dull reflections in dreamy states of woeful gleams—
She mourns my heart beyond the dark
but loses hope for me, it seems.

I've howled at the gods in my dreams
and I've clawed at the seams
of where the sky touches the tops of the leaves,
but nothing has changed…

Perhaps, my voice has been carried to her by now:

Though I will shrivel in age beneath the passing suns,
and though I will grow into a grave below the padded soils
simply
because I am bound by mortality,
my love for you will remain
immortal.

"I've clawed at the seams of where the sky touches the tops of the leaves"

il tuo nome

You remain hidden,
your name carved into the walls of my throat with volcanic glass;
you are
the age-worn book that I fear might crumble
if removed from its glass case
kept in the dark.

"you are"

Flower-walker

She was the queen of wildflowers;
when she walked
she woke the earth with the steps of Spring.

"the queen of wildflowers"

[Untitled, 2]

Bury me beneath the trees,
so that I may witness the stars swirl through the seasons.
Allow me to be showered on
by the dying rainbows of autumn leaves;
I believe,
only these beauties can calm my soul until you join me.

"Bury me beneath the trees"

Luna

We have sat together on the edge of the cliffside,
overlooking the Prussian blues
beyond the plunging breaks of the beach.

It was there your hair
covered the deepness of your stars as they rained down for us,
behind gentle waves of obsidian
that glimmered dark pearls in the night.

The silvers of your nightgown shimmered indigos
as it flowed in lyrical dance;
its delicate lace brushed against the heavy air
and exuded sadness for us.

"We have sat together on the edge of the cliffside"

Hands of God

What, if not amethyst hands
that have crafted cosmos,
hands creased violet with timelines,
could have created you?
What, if not fingertips forged
by celestial fire,
could have shaped you through starcluster-ceramics?

"that have crafted cosmos"

L'amour de ma vie

The stars can cut the tongue out from my mouth,
they can damn me to walk the world in silence
and still, in my muteness,
I would love you in whispers withheld.

I would walk the earth barefoot
and carve canyons with my steps so that waters could flow,
and you would know, *I love you.*

"and carve canyons with my steps so that waters could flow"

Library-eyes

I have walked the depths of the aisles in your eyes,
for they have drawn me deeply down.
I find
that I have found towers of dusted books
bound in point lace.
Your library ladder
offers vibrant whispers in its wheels,
and I am entranced.

My spirit dances in alchemy
and glows more golden than the veins of stars,
for I can read you.

"for they have drawn me deeply down"

Fever dream

There you lay before me,
the alabaster canvas of the gods
eager, to be painted with strokes of fervor.
The dark coffee of your silk hair
has spilled around the frame of your face in anticipation
of poetry with a pulse; poetry that is raw.

Your neck holds traces of a language translated in sweat,
the decrypted odes that escape you
taste of fever,
of desire, that echoes deep in your veins.

Milk-kissed thighs beckon my attention
but, I am entranced by the taste of liquid iron upon my lips,
born before the carnal lust of your thorny teeth
that bites into my flesh.
The inside of your cheeks
are painted in the red wine of my arteries;
You swish me slowly, and roll me over those ivory fangs
as you attempt to discern the nuances in my copper.

Our breath sharpens itself into small daggers
that stab at our stamina,
as we grind against the whetstone of ecstasy.

And when our throats can no longer contain the scream
of the frenzied hornets buzzing about,
we release from the fever dream
with
warm honey and waves of cellular napalm,
into a euphoric sonnet of humming orchestras.

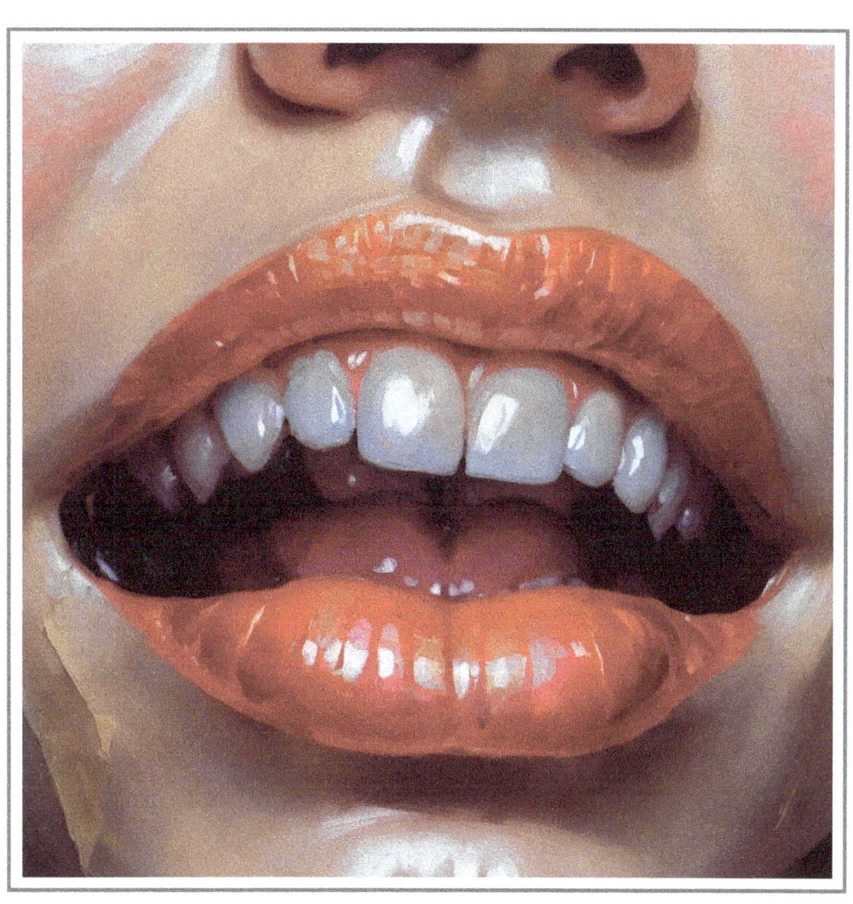

"and roll me over those ivory fangs"

Amaranthine love

You are lips of honey, eyes of fire
you are desire;
My heart plays harps for you.

"The fairest" the fairies say, as they
swoon and they sway in the midst of the midsummer dream.
And demigods and demons scheme
between the sutures and the seams of the world,
doting,
exploding with amaranthine love for *you.*

Words won't grasp what I need to say:

I vibrate cosmically in my connection to you,
my lovely viola d'amore.

"The fairest the fairies say"

Nefelibata

Yesterday, we crawled the caves
between the Blue Mountains and the yellow woods,
scraping by and slipping through the secrets in the stones;
It was there
we reached the edge,
of just how far we could run away.

I think
that maybe tomorrow we should scale the dormant mountain
to reach the snow-capped peaks,
perhaps
we might mix the ash with snow
and call it love.

"between the Blue Mountains and the yellow woods"

Red Thread

In the realm of lovers red,
fate fiddles with her lovely threads
and weaves her crimson knots.
She spins her webs as she embeds
our love in plots that lie ahead.

Fate's ties of red are bonding,
they're powerful, it's true.
They're stronger than the twisting
that the threads themselves will do.

If ever there's a time you find you need a sign,
trace that thread to me:

For in the realm of love and red our fate is tied, our path is led,
and I'll love you till we meet (again).

"In the realm of lovers red"

Between the stars

To the girl who drank the moon and ripped the sky,
who walked the oceans and who could fly
you are beautiful, yet this does not define
who you are.

You are the girl who dances with stars,
you are the one the night kisses.
You are the one with magic
deep
like the well with my wishes.

You say my name and the wind sings
to my heart.
How deep is your love? You ask.
The dark between the stars.

Your aura strikes awe into my bones.
When I hold you, I hold my home.

I love you wildly.

There are theories for everything and mine for us is this:
We are a love that always has
and always will exist

"The dark between the stars"

Just be

and in the glass we see:

"Please, if I plead, will you cease?
Will you release?
If I open this window will you at least believe?
Why won't you answer me?
I can see you from this mirror, you look like you agree.
So why be silent?
Why allow me to grieve?

Oh I see

perhaps you're finally going to let the flames
just be."

"you're finally going to let the flames
just be"

Why we swim

Through low-hanging fogs
that hover over blackened lagoons,
I paddle through poison seeking,
searching, for you.
I look past the monsters in my minds mist and
up
through the smog in which I drift,
for an answer that may not exist.

Why do we swim?

"that hover over blackened lagoons"

Sunflower

I dream of you
in sunflower fields as you walk through the stalks.
You search for the flower with wilting petals;
For the flower that is dying.

You brush away the strong stems
as you lift your camera.
You focus the lens on the lifeless flower with wilting petals;
On the flower that is dying.

The colors on your canvas come together
as you create your masterpiece.
You paint the flower with wilting petals;
The flower that is dying.

I dream of you in sunflower fields
as you cut the stem and head home.
You hang it upside down,
tying it, air drying it,
this flower with wilting petals;
This flower that is dying.

This is the one you want.

"I dream of you in sunflower fields"

Train car

I imagine you
in the empty seat down at the end of the train car.
The screaming of the iron wheels
falls deaf upon your ears,
as you sit, silently rocking with the tracks.

Your earthy eyes are caught in a dark book,
and you are quietly framed
in the gold light
that bursts through the window panes.

Small shimmers reflect around you
as dust in the air dances, for your attention.

Where are you going?

"in the empty seat down at the end of the train car"

Wild Geese

Start a fire with my bones
and play catch with the sounds of their crackles;
Cook those wild stars in your heart.

Beckon back to the wild geese
who cut through the night sky, who call to the winds
for us.
If I could trumpet back I would,
but my music has been drowned in the peculiar magic
of fear.

Perhaps,
I will be able to answer before the embers of my bones
have their faint glow, slowly, snuffed out.

"Cook those wild stars in your heart"

As always

I am yours today
as I was yesterday when you loved me—
completely.

"completely"

Broken Heart Soliloquy

Give me God's ear
and They will hear it without restraint!

How dare you–
craft my soul from earthy clays, yet bind my boots to concrete coffins.
My heart feels oceans, but can see no stars to navigate!
YOU.
You have flooded my veins, like wild rivers after a storm,
with glowing magma and called it love;
called it the gift of poetry!

You, are cruel.

Look me in my eyes God. And tell me.
Why?

Why does the sun burn itself alive?
Why does the air slip between the spaces in my fingers when I reach for it?
And why
does my love for her crush me
with mountains in my chest?

They say You made us in Your image
but, who am I really?

"but, who am I really?"

The next morning

I could not escape how dense the dying stars were
that
collapsed behind my chest and crushed my naked heart.
The time that passed in just one morning
tasted of bitter flower petals that warned of slow poison.
My splintered bones
had almost forgotten heartbreak, but here we are,
reminding them with knives and hammers.

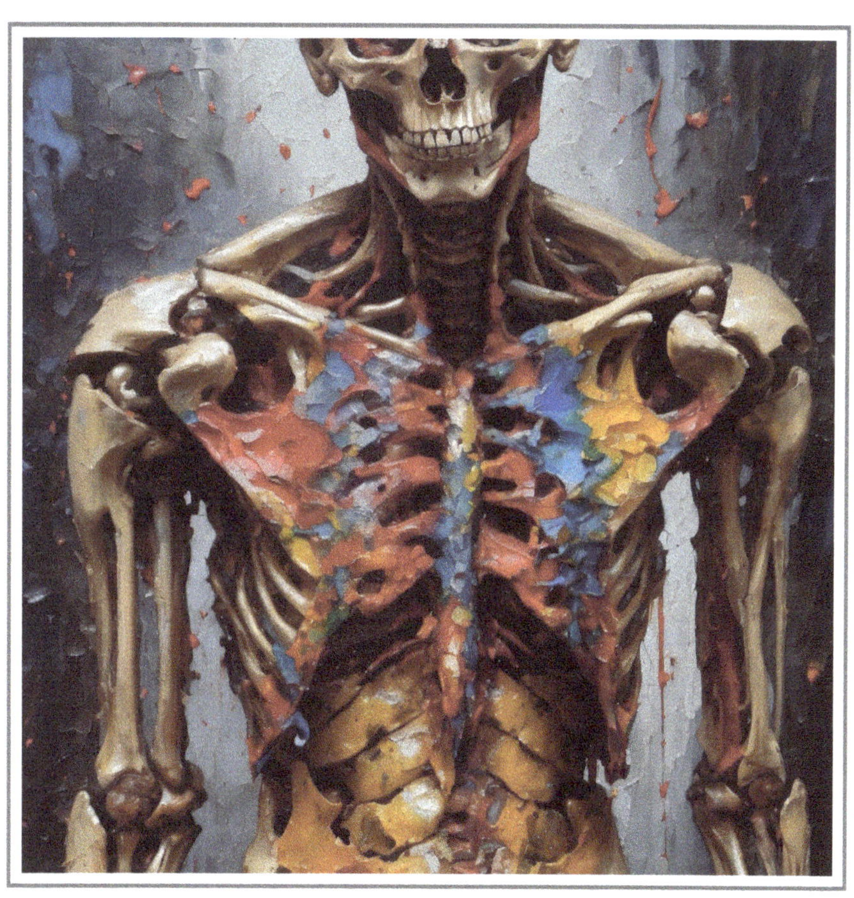

"had almost forgotten heartbreak, but here we are"

Wildfire

How tragic—
that my heart has erupted
and rained fire from my throat unto my body;
that I may walk the world ablaze
in agony,
with only my pen to dampen the flames.

"that I may walk the world ablaze"

Below the surface

I have been bolted down,
bound to the blackened depths of a drowned ocean floor;
of a damned seabed
long forgotten beneath the dark trenches.

Here,
in the water below the surface
I exist.

Do you see me?

"bound to the blackened depths"

Labyrinth

I feel certain that I am going mad, all alone.
You're getting close, the maze walls whisper,
as they shift when my eyes close.

Why must I balance myself on the bridge
between here and there?

We have all strayed so far from tribe and fire
that I think we may have forgotten—
We owe a great debt to the old lightning gods;
For they taught us how to stay warm
with ancient strikes against the dry plains.

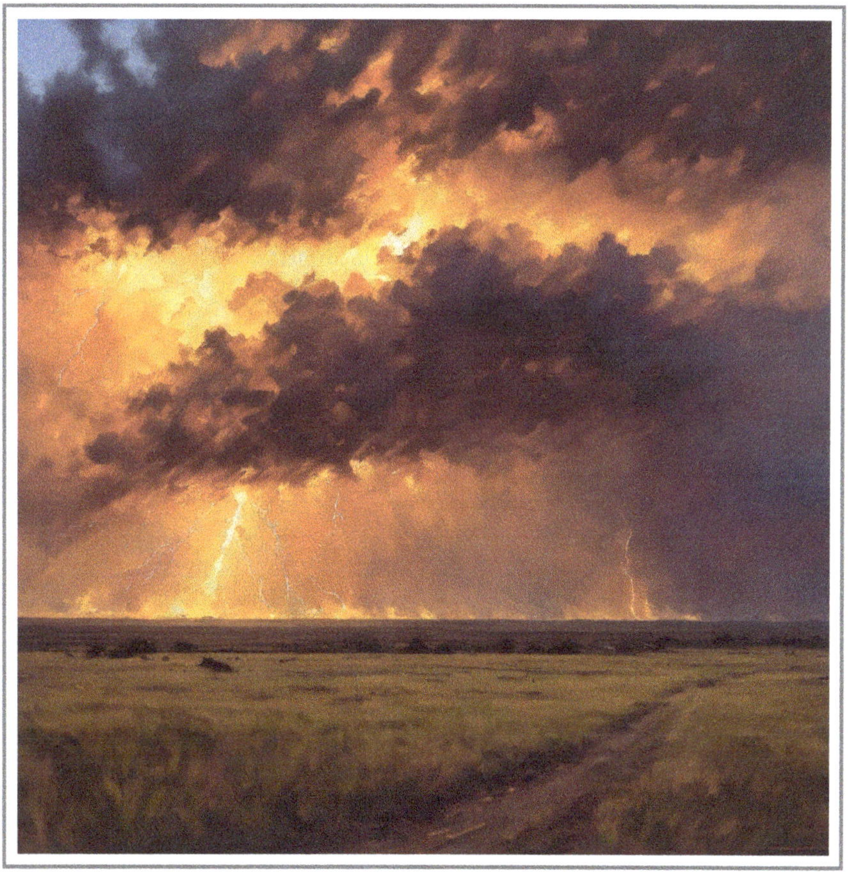

"with ancient strikes against the dry plains"

(???)

Give me thunder
that paints the woodsy air in rain,
that pelts against the tarps in cracking snaps;
Show me art
that rumbles against my name.

Rip me apart, oh Heavenly forest gale!
And tell me—
What was I called
when I was but atoms in stars?

"that pelts against the tarps in cracking snaps"

For Us

The silence in the shifting silt
screams at us to stop walking,
to stop treading along
and to stay just a moment longer,
to
take in the river deltas and the smooth stones
along the water spine.

But,
we can't do that can we?

What's left for us,
but to bathe beneath the showers of a red-rayed twilight,
as the hazy sun melts in heartbreak against the curve of the horizon
with poetic plums and deep oranges?

Perhaps
pianos and daydreams will keep us afloat
long after
the Ferryman sinks into the Styx,
and if the Spinner and her sisters decide differently,
then
let us live within these pages.

"as the hazy sun melts in heartbreak against the curve of the horizon"

"The centre of every poem is this:
I have loved you.
I have had to deal with that."

—Salma Deera, *Letters from Medea*

Thank you.

-D.